Geometric Drawing
and the
Waldorf School Plan

Geometric Drawing and the Waldorf School Plan

Hermann von Baravalle, Ph.D.

Waldorf Curriculum Series
Rudolf Steiner College Publications 1991

Geometric Drawing and the Waldorf School Plan
Hermann von Baravalle

Table of Contents

EQUIPMENT

For geometric drawing it is vital to have the proper equipment. Sheets of paper 12 x 18 inches are large enough to practice the various techniques well and still not too large for the average classroom desks. The principal instruments for geometric drawing are compasses and two drawing triangles. The compasses can be from simple pencil compasses to the best drawing sets, depending on the purpose of the work and the means available. Drawing triangles are used to draw parallel and perpendicular lines, as well as straight lines of different directions, particularly 45°, 30°, 60°, 90°. Drawing triangles of celluloid are recommended, one an isosceles triangle with the angles of 90°, 45°, 45° (the recommended size of the longest side between 12 and 15 inches) and the other, ½ of an equilateral triangle of the angles of 90°, 30°, 60° (the recommended size of the longest side between 12 and 15 inches). Should the expenditure for them be prohibitive, self made triangles, cut out of strong cardboard, can take their place.

Another tool is a ruler preferably with both inches- and centimeter-scales (we recommend wooden rulers, 12 inches long). Further materials are pencils and erasers. Geometric drawing pencils should be used exclusively for geometric drawing; they need to be sharpened with finer points than notebook pencils and would break if they were used for other purposes. We recommend No. 2 or No. 3 pencils (No. 1 are too soft and the carbon smears on the paper and the No. 4 are too hard and strain the eyes). The pencils should be of good quality. Two kinds of erasers are used for different purposes, a soft eraser (art gum, for instance) for erasing fine lines of construction and an ink eraser for making corrections of strongly drawn lines.

The drawings should not be bent or rolled. Each plate should be a carefully treated and well completed piece of work with a hand lettered heading (not handwriting). A heading lettered in large and small letters between three equally spaced horizontal lines produces the best results. The same script, only smaller, will be used for the name and the plate-number.

The use of color, colored pencils for lines and areas, or even water-color washes for areas, can bring out certain geometric elements much more clearly. Some students may find this difficult at the start, but it will bring them much satisfaction as they acquire the necessary skill through practice, patience and perseverance.

DIVISIONS OF A CIRCLE
POLYGONS AND STELLAR POLYGONS

The regular forms are a natural start for the study of geometric drawing. They are obtained by dividing a circle into equal parts. Such divisions are carried out with different constructions. These are done in part by means of a few simple construction lines and in part out of a rich mathematical background.

THE 6-DIVISION

The 6-division takes a special position among construction processes. It is constructed by opening the compass to the radius of the circle, the same measurement by which the circle itself was drawn.

The steps for dividing the circle into six equal parts are shown in the following diagrams (Figures 1-5).

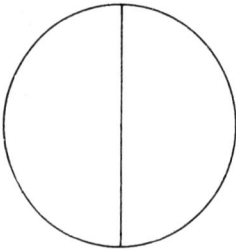
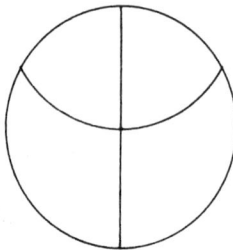
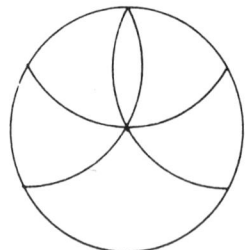

Figure 1   Figure 2   Figure 3

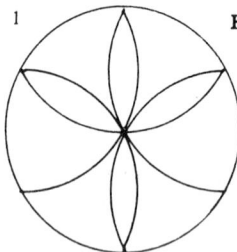
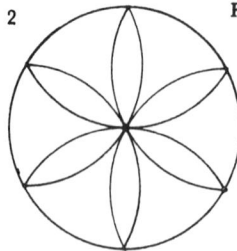

Figure 4   Figure 5

The 6-DIVISION of a CIRCLE.

The beginning of the construction is the same as in Figure 1 with a vertical diameter dividing the circle into two parts. Drawing triangles are used. One triangle is placed against the upper margin of the paper and the other is held against it as shown in Figure 6.

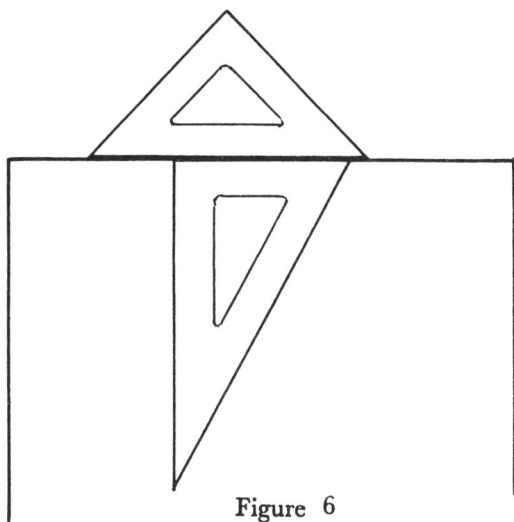

Figure 6

The vertical line marks the highest and lowest points on the circle. The compass needle is then placed in the highest point and an arc is drawn inside of the circle with the same radius as that of the circle (Figure 2). The arc intersects the circle at two points. These are used for the next positions of the compass needle. With their positions and the same radius, two further arcs are drawn within the circle (see Figure 3). These arcs again intersect the circle and furnish two additional intersection points in the lower half of the circle. These points are used once more as centers for the next arcs (Figure 4). Finally an arc is drawn from the lowest point of the circle, completing the diagram of Figure 5.

It is helpful for the student to be given the correct measurements on his paper. These are marked in inches for a 12 x 18 sheet. (Figure 7).

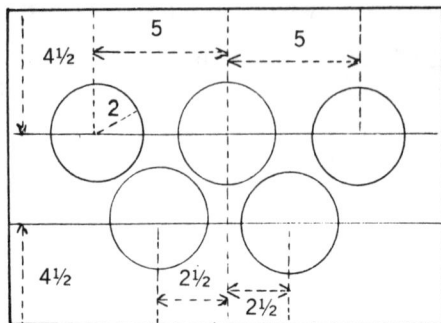

Figure 7

By extending the arcs in Figure 5 to full circles, one obtains Figure 8, showing a total of seven circles which are combined in the 6-division construction.

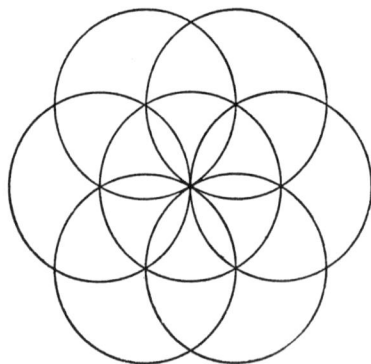

Figure 8
The seven circles of the 6-Division construction.

The special role of the 6-division of a circle can be shown by means of an experiment with coins. Taking seven coins of the same kind and arranging six coins about the seventh, one obtains the pattern of Figure 9. The coins fit perfectly together whether they are dimes, quarters or half-dollars.

12

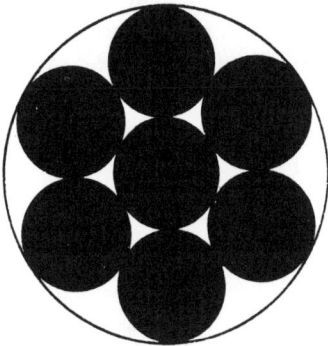

Figure 9
Arrangement of 7 circles

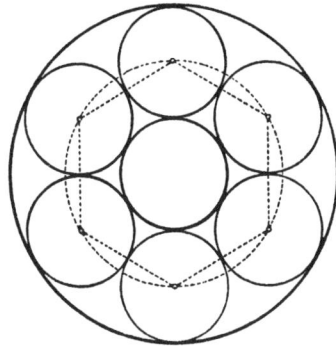

Figure 10
Drawing of combination of 7 circles

In Figure 10, the centers of the circles are marked and dotted lines are drawn between them. The distance between the centers of two circles which are tangent to one another is two radii. The construction of Figures 1-5 finds its explanation in the relationship of these circles.

By connecting the centers of the six circles or the points of any 6-division of a circle, one obtains a regular six-sided polygon, a hexagon (see Figure 11).

Figure 11
Regular hexagon

Figure 12
Stellar hexagon

Figure 13
Inner stellar hexagons

Figure 12 is drawn without the circles by just following the movements of the 6-divisions as before and leaving only traces behind. The points of the 6-division are then joined and one obtains the hexagon. In Figure 12 the same points are joined so that every point is connected with the second one following it along the circle. This results in a six-pointed star (stellar hexagon) inscribed in the hexagon.

13

The students may discover on their own that the central space left in the stellar hexagon is again a regular hexagon in which another stellar hexagon can be inscribed. In this manner one continues and can go on indefinitely. In every hexagon there is an inscribed stellar hexagon and in every stellar hexagon in turn, another hexagon (Figure 13). The measurements for a plate with the figures 11 to 13 are given in Figure 14.

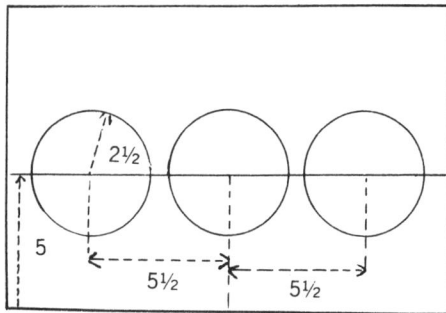

Figure 14

THE 12-DIVISION

From the 6-division of a circle one can continue to its 12-division. One way is drawn in Figure 15. It uses the same circles as in Figure 8 and proceeds by joining their points of interesection with the center of the diagram.

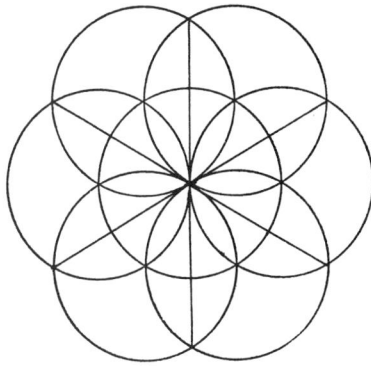

Figure 15
12-Division of a circle

Another way introduces the construction of bisecting an angle. Between two neighboring points of the 6-division of a circle as their centers, arcs are drawn with any equal radii, large enough to yield an intersection point between them. From this point a line is drawn to the center of the given circle. Where it cuts this circle is an additional point of the 12-division.

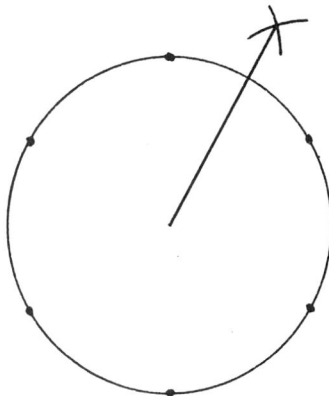

Figure 16
Bisecting an angle in proceeding from the
6-Division to the 12-Division of a circle.

Joining the points of a 12-division of a circle consecutively one obtains a 12 sided regular polygon, a dodecagon (Figure 17). Joining every second of these points (Figure 18), or every 3rd (Figure 19) or every 4th (Figure 20) or every 5th (Figure 21) or, finally, every 6th (Figure 22) one obtains different stellar polygons.

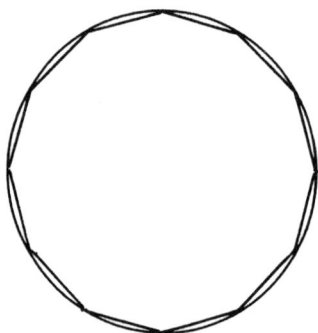

Figure 17

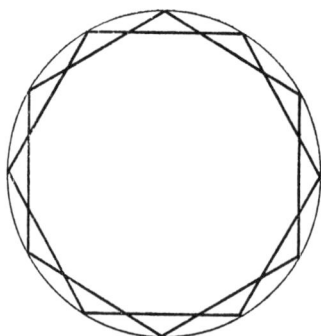

Figure 18

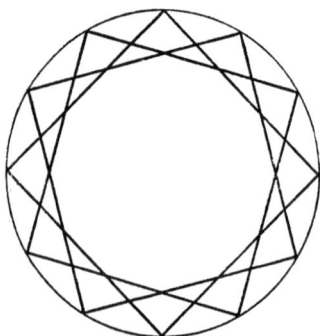

Figure 19

Figure 20

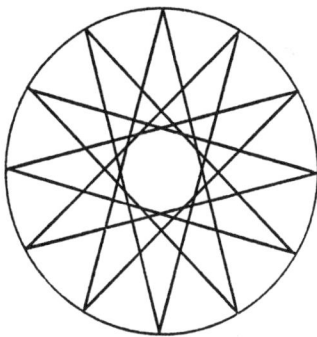

Figure 21

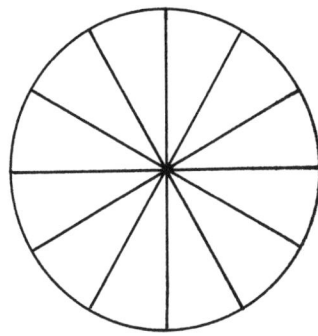

Figure 22

*The different stellar
dodecagons*

Joining the 7th, 8th, 9th, 10th, or 11th points brings one again back to the same diagrams. The stellar dodecagon of Figure 18 is composed of two interlaced hexagons, the one of Figure 19 of three interlaced squares and of Figure 20 of four interlaced equilateral triangles. The stellar dodecagon of Figure 21 is a continuous line. On its completion it returns to its point of departure. In Figure 22, the dodecagon dissolves into six diameters.

To arrange a plate of the dodecagons on a 12 x 18 sheet the measurements are marked in Figure 23.

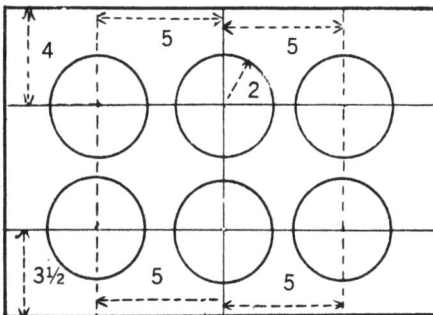

Figures 2 3

There are number relationships connected with the different stellar polygons. If the two determining numbers, that of the vertices of the

17

polygon and that of the steps spanned by the connecting lines (with Figure 18, for instance: 12 and 2) have a factor in common (with Figure 18 the factor is 2) the total stellar polygon dissolves into two or more separated polygons. If the determining numbers have no factors in common besides the self-evident "one" (in Figure 21: 12 and 5) the stellar polygon is a continuous line.

THE 24-DIVISION

Bisecting the arcs between the points of a 12-division of a circle one arrives at a 24-division. Joining its points consecutively one obtains a 24 sided regular polygon. Joining every second, third, fourth, etc., of these points various 24 sided stellar polygons result. Drawing them all, one obtains a 24 sided regular polygon with all its diagonals (Figure 24).

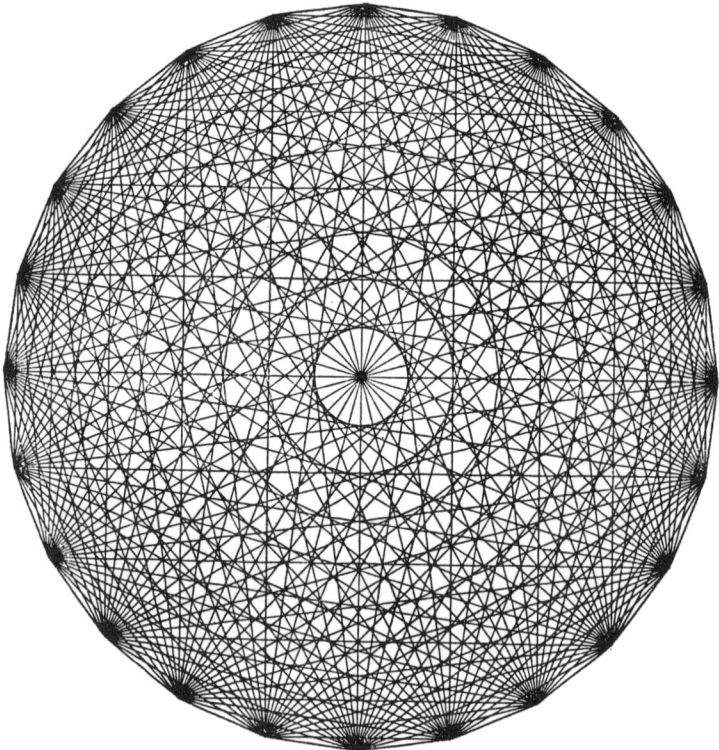

Figure 24
24 sided polygon with all diagonals

For a plate with the 24 sided polygon on a 12 x 18 sheet the measurements are given in Figure 25.

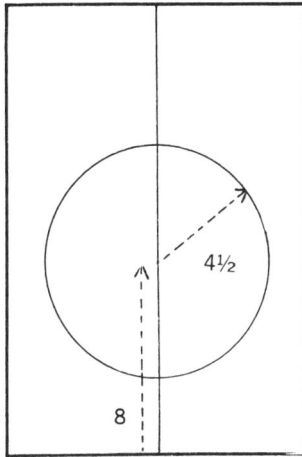

Figure 25

VARIOUS DIVISIONS INCLUDING 5 AND 7

Further divisions with their respective regular polygons and stellar polygons are described with the following diagrams. The 2-division of the circle is completed by drawing a diameter (contained in Figure 26). The 3-division is part of the 6-division and is completed by a diameter and one arc (see Figure 26). The center of the arc is the lower end of the vertical diameter and its radius is the same as the radius of the given circle. The 4-division is carried out by the vertical and horizontal diameters (see Figure 27).

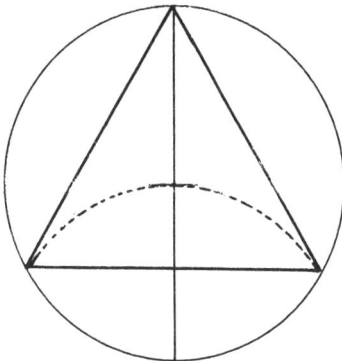

Figure 26

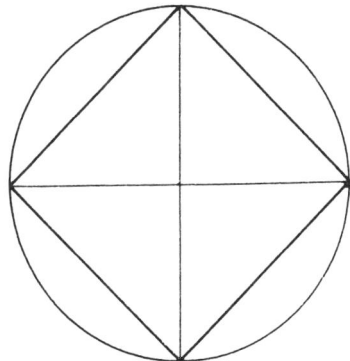

Figure 27

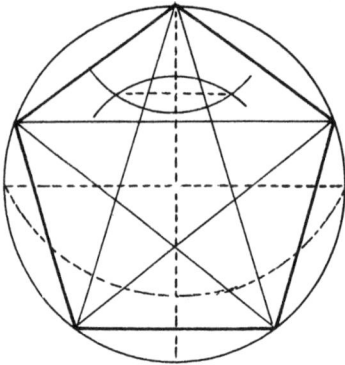

Figure 28

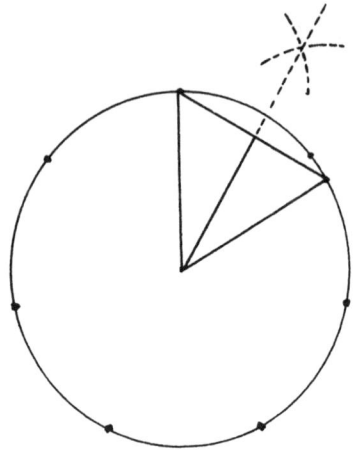

Figure 29

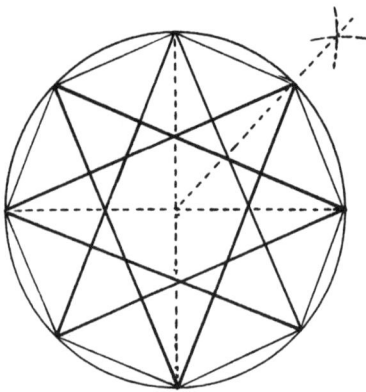

Figure 30

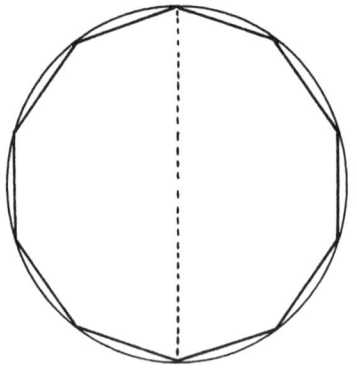

Figure 31

Various divisions of a
circle

The 5-division of a circle has its mathematical background in the Golden Section (compare the article by the author in "The Mathematics Teacher", Vol. XVI No. 1). Its construction is an absolute construction; it is correct to all decimals of its measurements. Its lines are shown as dotted lines in Figure 28. The circle with its vertical and horizontal diameters is drawn first. Then one bisects the upper radius of the vertical diameter and places the compass-needle in its mid-point. The compass is opened to one of the end points of the horizontal diameter and an arc is described inside of the circle. The distance of its point of intersection with the vertical diameter from one of the end points of the horizontal diameter equals the side of a pentagon, inscribed in the circle. Taking this length on the compass and cutting it off on the circle from the upper end of the vertical diameter to right and left yields the two points which — together with the upper end of the vertical diameter — are three points of the pentagon. The rest of its points are obtained with the aid of another measurement which is also taken from the described arc. It is the distance from the lowest point of the arc to the center of the original circle. Taking it on the compass and cutting it off on the circle from its lowest point to the right and left one gets the fourth and fifth points of the pentagon. By connecting the five pentagon points consecutively one obtains a regular pentagon. Connecting every second of these points one gets a stellar pentagon (see Figure 28).

In Figure 29, is shown the 7-division of a circle. This is an approximate construction and gives the length of the side of a regular seven-sided polygon, the regular heptagon. The accuracy is sufficient to make Figure 29 as good as an absolute construction. The lines of construction are partly drawn as dotted lines. The sides of the regular heptagon equal the altitude of an equilateral triangle whose sides are the radius of the circle. The heptagon side is then cut off from the highest point of the given circle three times along the circle to the right and to the left.

The 8-division of a circle (see Figure 30) is effected by bisecting the arcs between the four end-points of the vertical and horizontal diameters. The diagram shows the regular octagon and the stellar octagon connecting every third point.

The 10-division of a circle (see Figure 31) can be obtained by bisecting the arcs between the 5-division points or by applying again the length which had been used in the 5-division for obtaining the last two points of the pentagon.

TRISECTION OF AN ANGLE

For further divisions of the circle it is also useful to have a construction for the tri-section of an angle. In the following diagram the construction of Viète is described (Figure 32).

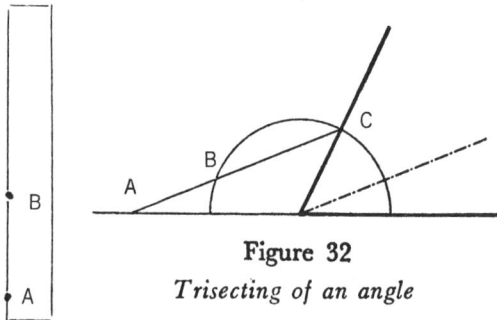

Figure 32

Trisecting of an angle

The angle which is to be trisected is drawn in stronger lines. About its vertex is drawn a semi-circle with any chosen radius, placed as in Figure 32. The length of its radius is also marked on the edge of a piece of paper (AB to the left of Figure 32). The piece of paper is then taken up and placed on the diagram in such a way that three conditions are met:

1. The point A lies on the prolonged diameter of the semi-circle.
2. The point B lies on the semi-circle.
3. The edge of the paper passes through point C, the point of intersection of the semi-circle and the inclined leg of the angle.

The line ABC will thus occupy a determined position, which holds a distinct angle against the horizontal. A line parallel to its direction drawn through the vertex of the given angle is drawn in dots and dashes. It cuts off exactly 1/3 of the given angle.(*)

---

* The proof for the trisection-construction proceeds as follows: The given angle is CMD in Figure 33. AM is a prolongation of MD. The placing of the line ABC following the trisection construction makes AB = MD = MC by construction. The points B and M are joined by a dotted line: BM is also equal to MC, to MD and to AB. In the triangle ABM, being isosceles, the two angles on the base are equal (marked with single arcs). The marked angle at B is is an exterior angle of the triangle ABM and therefore equal to the sum of its non-adjacent interior angles, to 2 single-arc-angles.

It is marked with a double arc. In the triangle BCM, being also isosceles, the two base angles are equal; both are marked with double arcs. This angle also equals the angle marked with double arcs at M, an alternate interior angle.

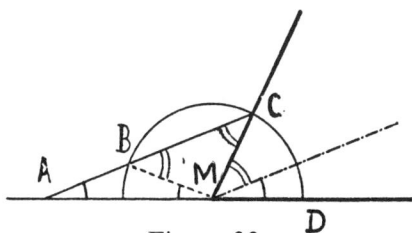

Figure 33
Proof of the trisection
construction

The given angle CMD is therefore the sum of the two angles, one marked with a single arc and one with a double arc; it equals 3 single-arc-angles.

Occasionally the statement is heard that one cannot trisect an angle. This means to say: Using only an unmarked ruler and a compass one cannot trisect an angle. The previous construction uses a marked straight edge but is just as exact as a construction with straight lines and arcs only.

EXPERIMENTING WITH PAPER CUTOUTS OF POLYGONS

Among the qualities of stellar polygons the following may be mentioned: When a five-sided stellar polygon is cut out of paper and the outer parts are bent inside (see Figure 34) another stellar pentagon is obtained within the central area.

Holding the folded paper before a light, one will see the whole stellar pentagon in the inner part of the cut as darkened areas. Each one of the triangles which have been bent over reaches exactly the opposite vertex of the inner pentagon. The experiment invites the question whether this fact will repeat itself with other stellar polygons. With the stellar hexagon of Figure 35 we find that the stellar triangles when bent inside no longer reach the opposite vertices of the central area but all meet in the center. The bent parts of the paper held before a light do not reproduce the six-sided polygon but evenly cover the central area (Figure 35). By cutting out a seven-sided stellar polygon (stellar heptagon) which has been drawn by connecting each point of a 7-division of a circle with the third one and by bending its outer triangles inside, we obtain a new inner stellar heptagon (Figure 36).

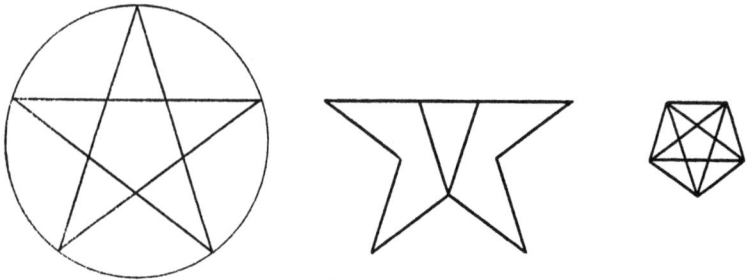

Figure 34
*Experimenting with paper cuts
of polygons*

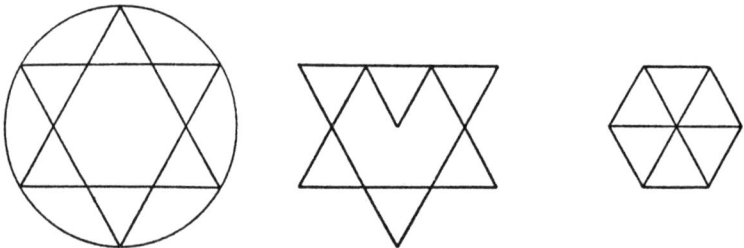

Figure 35
Bending a stellar hexagon

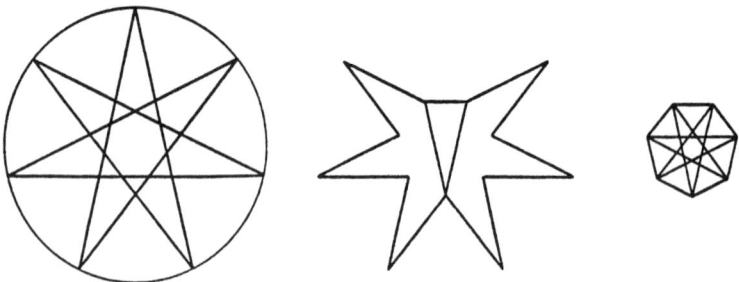

Figure 36
Bending a stellar heptagon

The same occurs with stellar polygons of 9, 11, 13, 15 sides, which have been drawn by connecting the 4th, 5th, 6th, 7th points respectively (in general with every 2n + 1-sided polygon drawn by connecting the nth points).

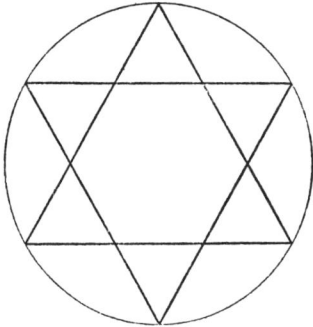 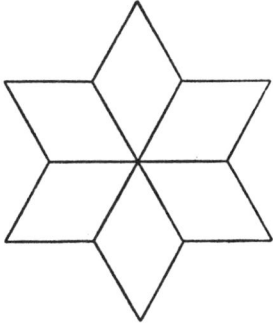

Figure 37

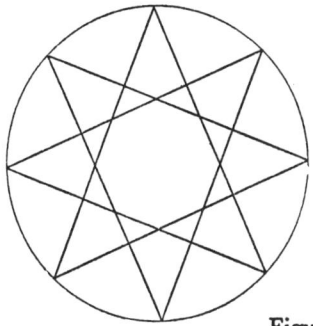 

Figure 38

Figure 39

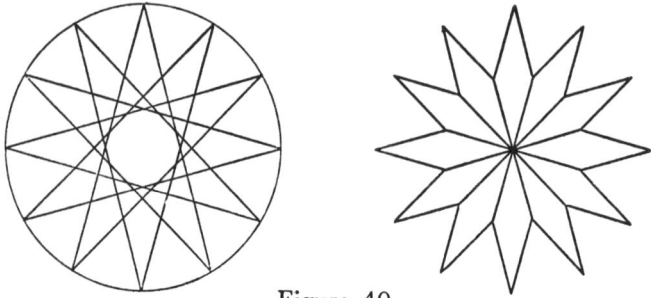

Figure 40

The stellar polygons of 8, 10, 12, 14 sides which are obtained by connecting every point with the 3rd, 4th, 5th, 6th one [stellar polygons of 2n sides drawn by connecting the (n—1)th points] show the same quality as the six-sided stellar polygon. The stellar triangles bent inside reach the center and evenly cover the central area. These facts are illustrations showing the contrast between the even and odd numbers.

PRACTICAL APPLICATION

A practical application of stellar polygons is the compass-pattern which is used in navigation and found on boats and planes, as well as on maps. It is obtained from a stellar polygon of sixteen points which connects every seventh point (see Figure 41) and by omitting certain line-segments in order to provide a primary emphasis on the four directions, North, South, East and West and a secondary emphasis on the directions between them (NORTHEAST = NE, SE, SW and NW) as seen in Figure 42.

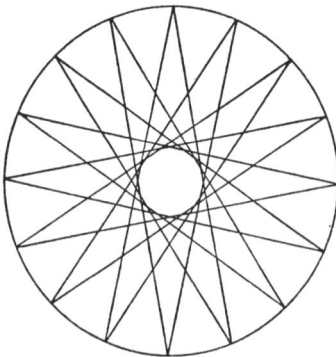

Figure 41
Sixteen-sided stellar polygon

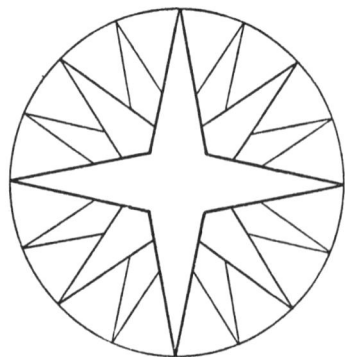

Figure 42
Compass pattern

GEOMETRIC PROGRESSION
AND EXPERIMENTS WITH PAPER CUTOUTS

From the constructions of regular polygons one can proceed to sequences of polygons. Figure 43 starts with its outer equilateral triangle.

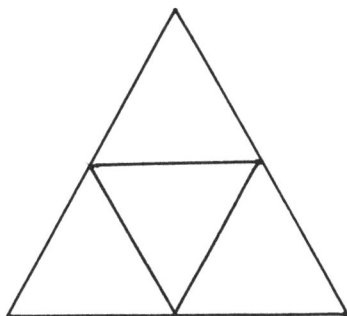

Figure 43
Inscribed triangles

There are various ways of constructing an equilateral triangle. Using compasses one may proceed with a 3-division of a circle as in Figure 26. Or, using only a drawing triangle with the angles of 90°, 60° and 30° one may start with the base and apply the angle of 60° at each end of the base, getting the inclined sides of the triangle. Their intersection point is the top of the triangle. Another way starts with the base, but then takes its length in the compass, places the needle at its end points and draws arcs. The arcs intersect at the top of the equilateral triangle. If the compass should not be large enough to span the total length of the base, one can proceed as in Figure 43 and take into the compass half the length of the base. Thus one first gets the tops of the 2 small triangles above the base. From them, putting another triangle on top, one reaches the large triangle. Still another way, makes use of the altitude of the equilateral triangle, etc.

After the outer triangle of Figure 43 is drawn, one finds the midpoints of its sides. This is a task of bisecting given line segments. Various ways can again be followed. One of them uses a ruler with inches or centimeters. Another one transfers the length to the edge of a paper and folds it over. The most precise way proceeds with a compass as seen in Figure 44.

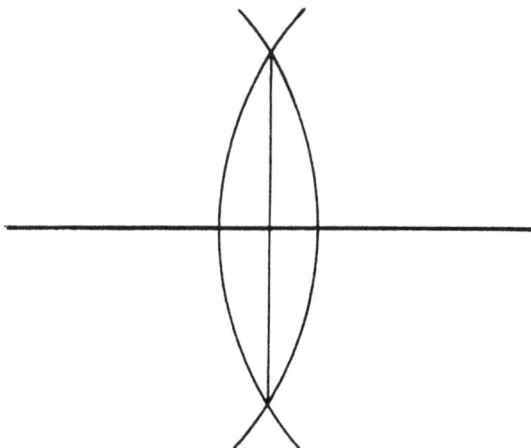

Figure 44
Bisecting a line-segment

Opening the compass to a span larger than half the given length and placing the compass needle first on one and then on the other end point one draws arcs 'with any radius, as in Figure 44. The straight line connection between the points of intersection of the arcs cuts the line segment at its mid-point.

By joining the midpoints ôf the three sides of the triangle in Figure 43, one obtains an inscribed triangle. Though a side of the inner triangle equals one-half of the side of the outer one, its area is only one-quarter of the area of the outside triangle. At this point one may raise the question: Does this relationship of one-half of the length and one-quarter of the area hold good for equilateral triangles only? First one will show that it holds good for any triangle, whatever its form might be. Figure 45 shows it for an acute, a right and an obtuse triangle. What about other forms? For a square it is immediately evident. How about a hexagon? Can one divide it into four hexagons of half the length of a side?

28

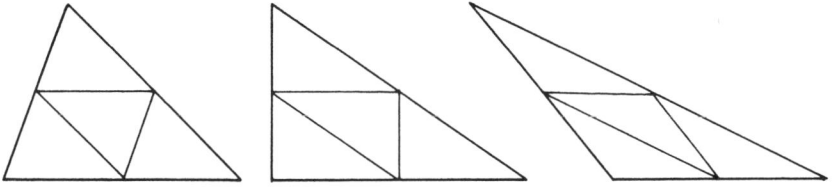

Figure 45
*Dividing various triangles
into four equal parts*

In Figure 46, two of the four hexagons are drawn in black and the remaining areas are composed of twice six equilateral triangles, forming two hexagons. Finally, one may mention that this relationship prevails for any form, whether composed of straight lines or even of curves.

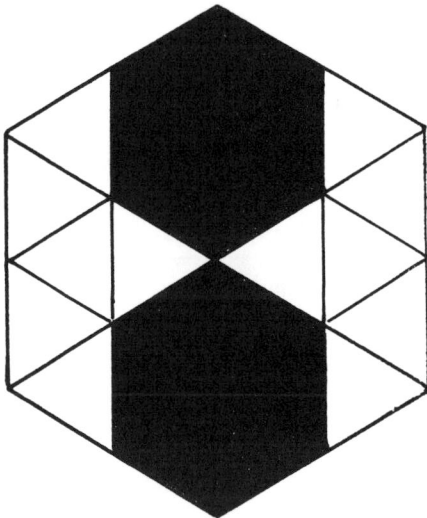

Figure 46
*Four hexagons of half the
side length*

29

If this construction of inscribed equilateral triangles is continued, each time joining the mid-points of the three sides of the preceding triangle, one obtains a geometric progression.

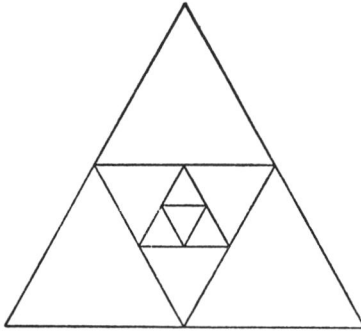

Figure 47
*Geometric progression of
equilateral triangles*

In the same way geometric progressions can be obtained for any polygon. For squares, for instance, this is drawn in Figure 48.

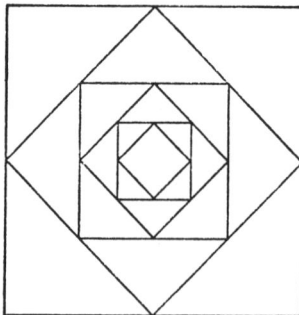

Figure 48
*Geometric progression of
squares*

Comparing Figure 47 and Figure 48 one notices how much more slowly the squares diminish than the triangles. The higher the number of the vertices of polygons, the slower is the process of the diminishing geometric progression. Another example is given in Figure 49 with a geometric progression of hexagons.

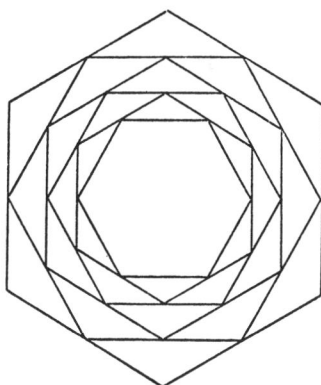

Figure 49
Geometric progression of hexagons

Joining the mid-points of the sides is not the only way to set up geometric progressions with polygons. In Figure 50, for instance, the sides of the squares have been divided into quarters. Any other fractions could also be used.

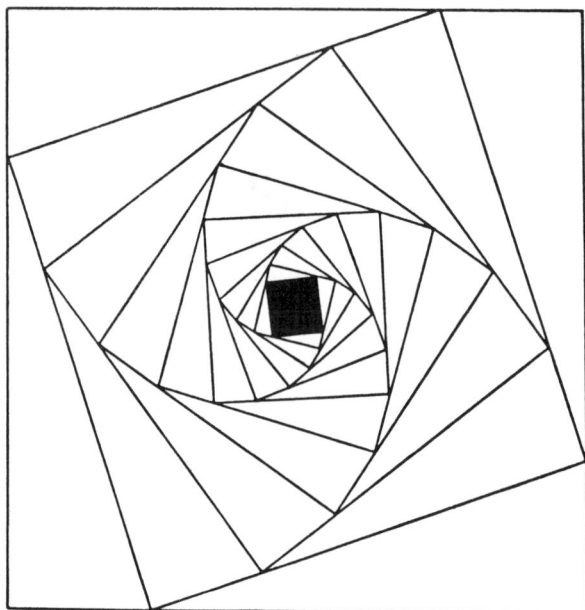

Figure 50
*Inscribed squares joining points at
one-quarter of the sides of the
previous squares*

Instead of using single polygons as members of a geometric progression one can also work with combinations of them. Figure 51 uses rings of twelve squares.

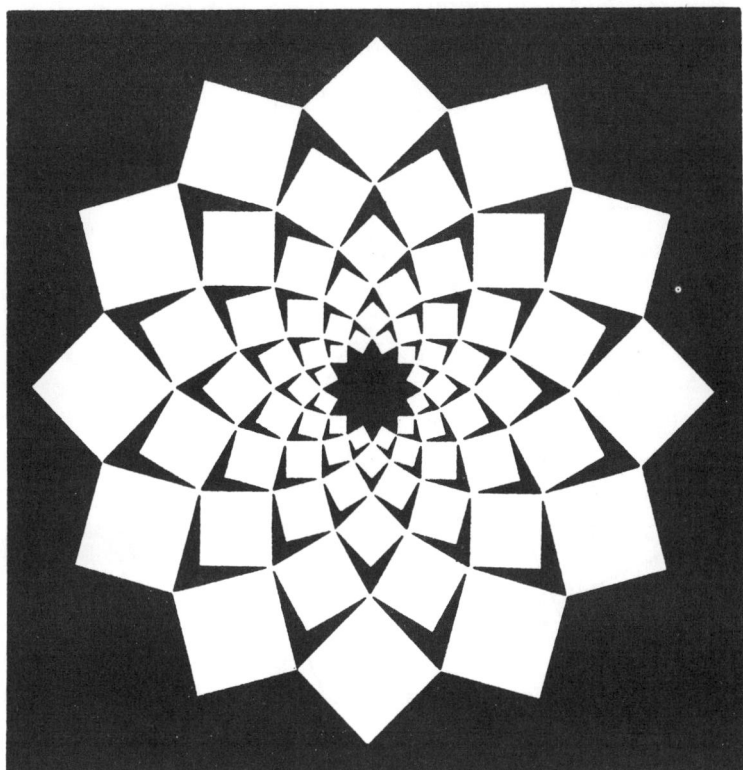

Figure 51
Geometric progression of
rings of squares

The diagram starts by dividing a circle into twenty-four equal parts. Connecting every second of the points of division and drawing prolonged radii through the rest of them one obtains the diagonals of the squares of the outer ring. The squares are drawn by making the four distances from the center to the four vertices equally long. From one ring one proceeds to the next inner one by repeating the construction in the same way. Geometric progressions of this kind are found in organic structures, on the back of pine cones, on the central part of sun flowers, etc.

Experiments with geometric progressions can also be carried out through paper cutouts. Taking a sheet of writing paper 8½ x 11 inches, folding it over along the medians and afterwards once more along a 45° line, one gets a wedge-like shape of fold. (See Figure 52).

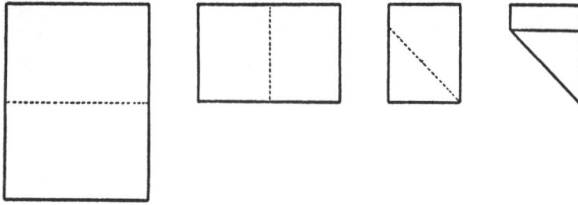

Figure 52
Folding paper

One holds it with the center of the sheet downward and draws lines on it as in figure 53. Finally, cutting through all eight layers of paper so that only the white parts of the last diagram remain, and after unfolding. one obtains the form of Figure 54.

Figure 53

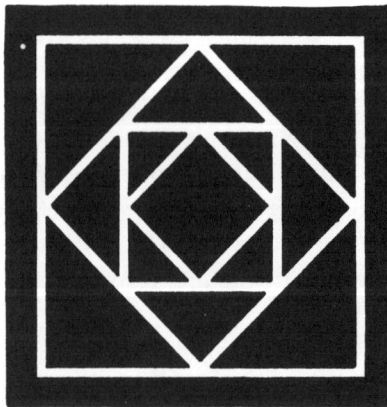

Figure 54
Geometric progression of squares cut out of paper

Similar operations with folding paper wedges of 30° and 22½° yield geometric progressions of hexagons and of octagons (see Figures 55 and 56).

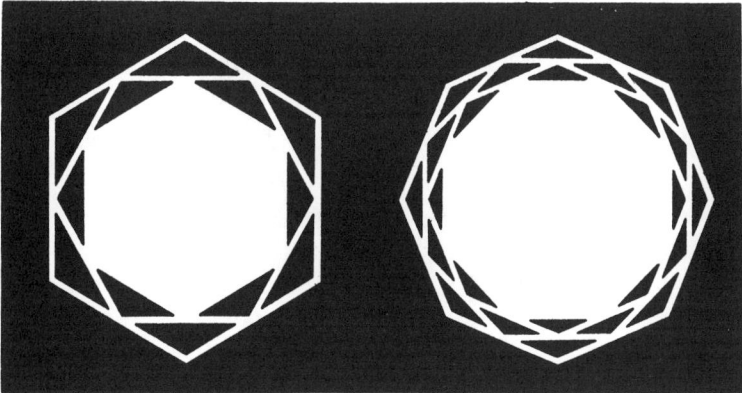

Figure 55   Figure 56
*Paper cutouts of geometric
progressions of hexagons
and octagons*

Stellar polygons can also be obtained through paper cutouts. The stellar dodecagon with three interlaced squares, for instance, can be made with a twelve fold paper wedge of 30° by drawing the line AB on it (first diagram of Figure 57) and the symmetrical line DE (second diagram of Figure 57). Then these lines are turned into double lines (third diagram of Figure 57) and cut out (fourth diagram of Figure 57). After unfolding, one obtains the stellar dodecagon of the three interlaced squares of Figure 58.

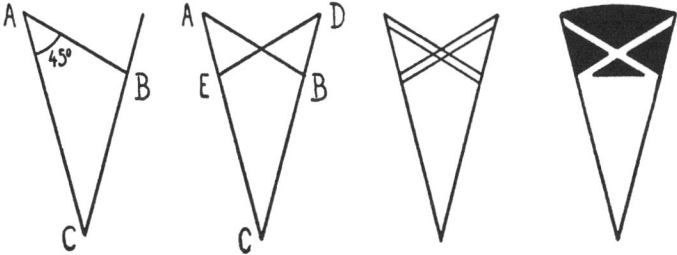

Figure 57
Making a stellar polygon by folding paper

Figure 58
Stellar dodecagon of three inter-
laced squares as paper cutout

The stellar dodecagon with four interlaced equilateral triangles also comes forth from a twelve-folded paper wedge of 30°. The broken line ABD is drawn on it (first diagram of Figure 59) and then a symmetrical line (second diagram of Figure 59). Then the single lines are turned into double lines (third diagram of Figure 59). Cutting them out, as shown in the fourth diagram of Figure 59, and unfolding, one obtains Figure 60.

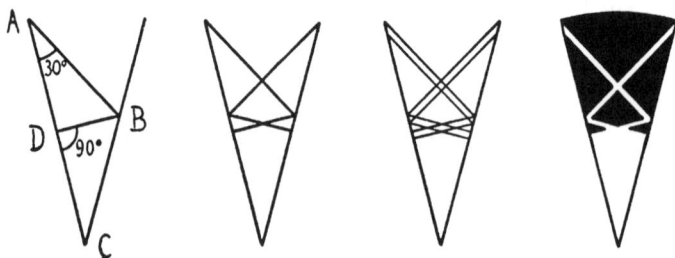

Figure 59
Construction of a
Stellar dodecagon of four
equilateral triangles
as paper cutout

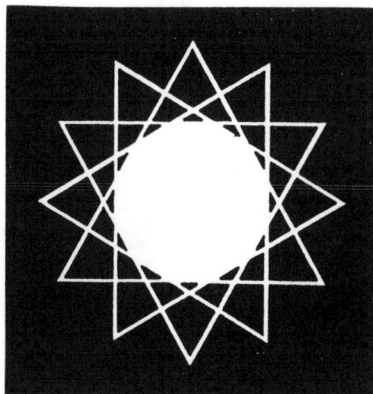

Figure 60

Some students show much more skill with paper cutouts than on the drawing board or in other class-work. The more we vary the media with which we work, the more we call upon different latent talents and interests in our students.

LOGARITHMIC SPIRALS

Taking up the geometric progression as in Figure 48 and emphasizing the areas between the lines alternately in black and white one can arrive at the diagram of Figure 61.

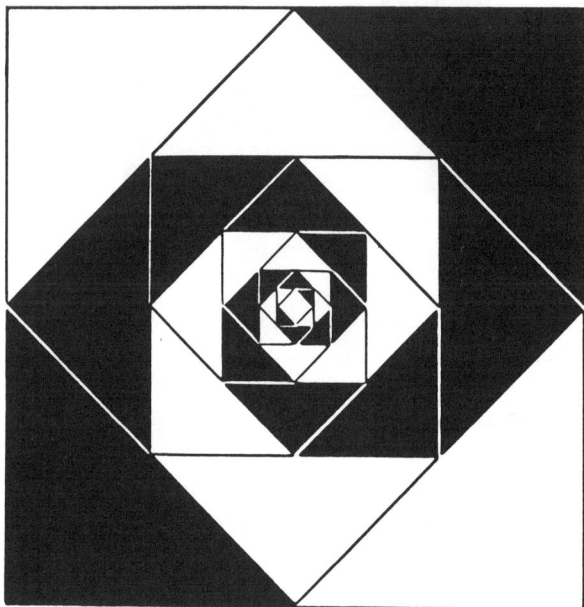

Figure 61
*Logarithmic spirals in a
geometric progression*

It shows the close connection between certain lines called logarithmic spirals and geometric progressions. Such lines are formed of half-sides of the successive squares. The name "logarithmic" refers to their connection with the sequence: $10^1 = 10$; $10^2 = 100$; $10^3 = 1000$, etc. $1 = \log 10$; $2 = \log 100$; $3 = \log 1000$, etc. The exponents grow in arithmetic progression and the numbers ten; hundred; thousand . . . in geometric progression. The exponents are called the logarithms of the numbers ten; hundred, thousand . . . In the logarithmic spirals the central angles grow in equal steps of $45°$, whereas the lengths and areas grow in geometric progressions.

Analogous treatment of hexagons leads to figure 62. and for octagons to Figure 63.

Figure 62
*Logarithimic spirals with geometric
progressions of hexagons*

Two families of logarithmic spirals make their appearance also with the geometric progression of the rings of twelve squares (Figure 51).

The construction of logarithmic spirals without polygons can be done in the following way: A circle is divided into a number of equal parts, in Figure 64 into twenty-four parts and the radii are drawn through all points of division. Then, starting with the top point of the circle a perpendicular is drawn to the following radius (see Figure 64), etc.

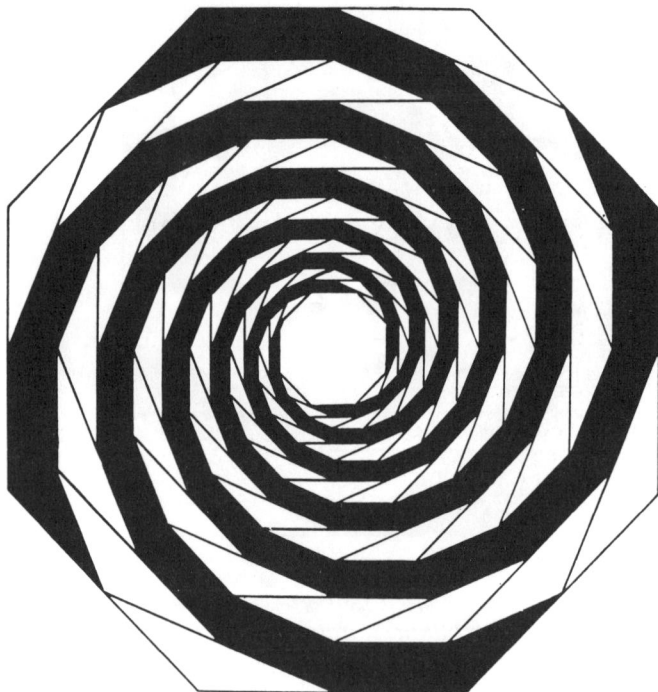

Figure 63
*Logarithmic spirals with geometric
progresions of octagons*

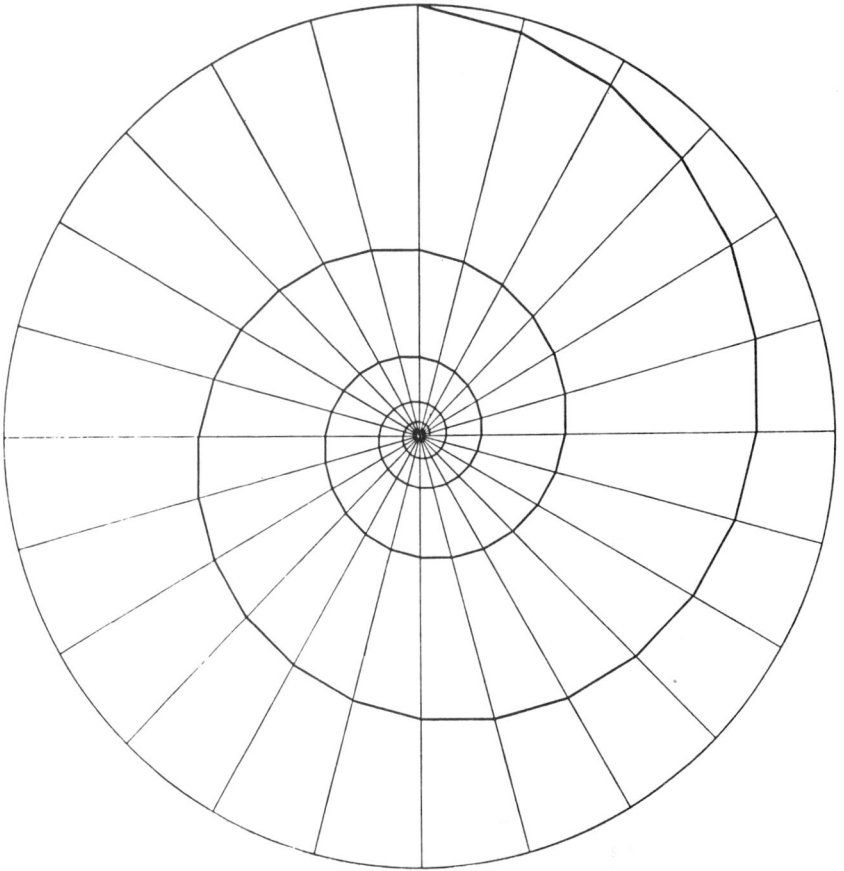

Figure 64
*Construction of the logarithmic
spiral with a 24 Division of
a circle*

The perpendiculars form a sequence of cords of the logarithmic spiral. By connecting the foot points by means of a curve the spiral appears as a continous line, instead of a line broken into straight-line segments. In Figure 65 this is done with a 12-division of a circle.

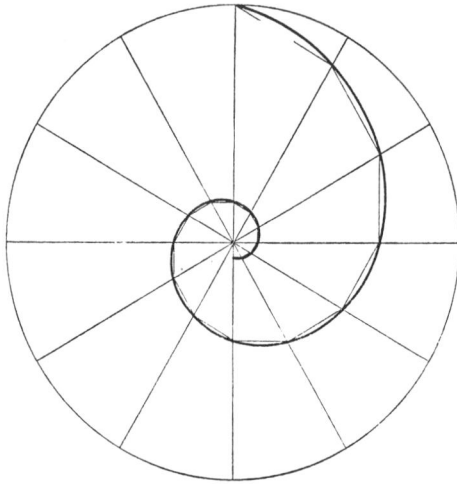

Figure 65
The logarithmic spiral drawn
as continuous curve

Logarithmic spirals appear frequently in nature. An example is the shell of the nautilus.

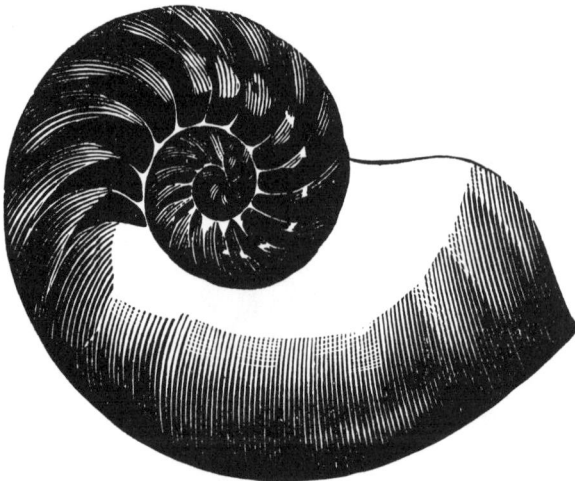

Figure 66
The nautilus shell

In Figure 66, the nautilus shell is seen cut in half as it is exhibited in the shell museum of Rollins College in Winter Park, Florida. There could be no better description of the geometry of spirals than that in the poem of Oliver Wendell Holmes, 'The Chambered Nautilus.' The animal in the shell proceeds from chamber to chamber as it grows in a geometric progression. The logarithmic spiral is indeed the geometric expression of organic growth.

THE SPIRAL OF ARCHIMEDES
AND THE CONSTRUCTION OF LEAF FORMS

The logarithmic spiral can be contrasted to another spiral which is connected with an arithmetic progression in the same way that the logarithmic spiral is with a geometric one. Its discovery goes back to antiquity to Archimedes and it has the name Spiral of Archimedes. In Figure 67 it is shown with a 16-division of a circle. Its points are obtained by moving from radius to radius in equal steps towards the center. The spiral starts at the periphery of the circle. On the next radius it is a certain distance inside the circle. This distance can be chosen at will; but once it is chosen the other points are determined, for the curve will be on the second radius twice this distance inside the circle, on the third three times this distance etc., until the length of the radius is exhausted and the curve ends at the center. When sailors aboard ship wind up the ropes, these form spirals of Archimedes. In a smaller scale all record discs have spirals of Archimedes pressed in, along which the needle glides.

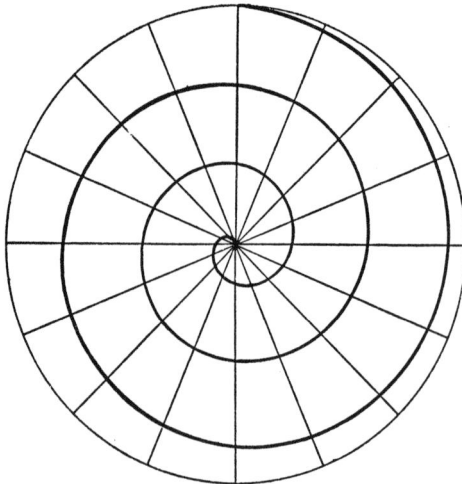

Figure 67
Spiral of Archimedes

With the aid of spirals one can construct various forms of leaves. The contour of a leaf displays a sequence of distances of its points from the point on which the leaf grows. In general, the tip of the leaf has the greatest distance from it. The distances then decrease on both sides of the edge until they finally come to zero. The process of decreasing can follow many different functions. The simplest is the decreasing by equal steps. Figure 68 shows 16 equal arcs around a circle. Among the 16 radii one points upwards to the tip of the leaf.

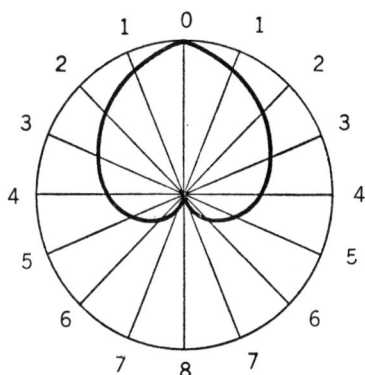

Figure 68

Leaf form from a circle

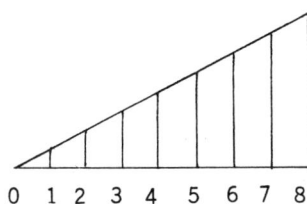

Figure 69

Its distance from the center is the full radius of the circle. On the other radii, the distances get smaller. The lengths which have been subtracted from the full radii follow the sequence of the vertical lines in the Figure 69 of the corresponding numbers. From point 0 in Figure 68, no length is subtracted. From the radii through the points number 1 in Figure 68 the lengths above point number 1 in Figure 69 have been subtracted. From the radii through the points number 2 in Figure 68 the lengths above point number 2 in Figure 69 have been subtracted, etc until from the radius through point 8 in Figure 68 the lengths above point eight in Figure 69 are subtracted. This is its total length. The resulting curves are spirals of Archimedes.

Proceeding to an equilateral triangle and carrying out an analogous construction we obtain Figures 70 and 71.

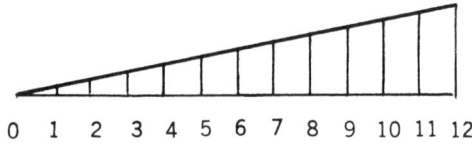

Figure 70

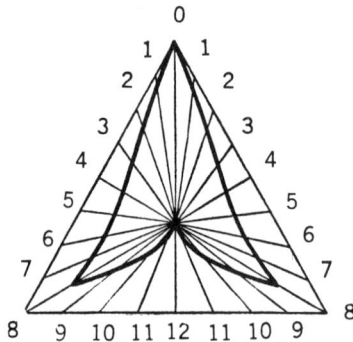

Figure 71

*Construction of a
leaf-form from
an equilateral triangle*

Every side of the triangle has been divided into eight parts (any divisions could have been used, but the 8-Division is particularly convenient). Thus the circumference received 24 points of division and half the circumference at each side received twelve points. The points of division have been connected with the center and numbered. The connecting lines are not of equal length. The latter only prevails with a circle and only with a circle is the term radii generally used. Applying it here also to other figures we can say: Only the top radius of the triangle has a maximum length. The opposite radius in the direction downwards (in Figure 71) is one-half the length of the top radius. This length is transferred to Figure 71 as the altitude above point 12 in Figure 70. The altitudes of the other points are gradually diminishing, 1/12 above point 1, 2/12 above point 2 and so forth. These are the lengths which will be subtracted from the respective radii of the triangle in Figure 71 to arrive at the leaf form. From the radii of the points 1 in Figure 71 the length above point 1 of Figure 70 is subtracted; from the radii of the points 2 in Figure 71 the length above point 2 in Figure 70 is subtracted, etc.

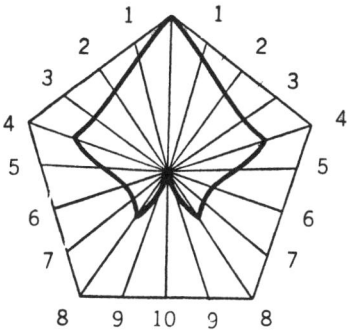

Figure 72

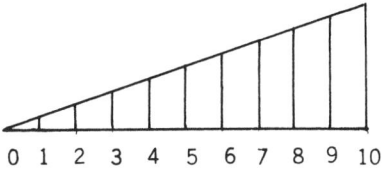

Figure 73

Leaf form from a pentagon

The analogous construction with a pentagon leads to Figures 72 and 73. Its form shows considerable resemblance to an ivy leaf.

ROTATION UPON ROTATION
EXERCISES WITH CIRCLES

The dotted circle in Figure 74 is divided into 24 parts and the points of division are marked with small rings. These points are the centers of circles of equal radii. The radii can be chosen at will. The resulting diagram shows the movement of a circle when its center is carried along another circle. The ancients spoke of epicycles (cycles upon cycles) and this became the key of their astronomy.

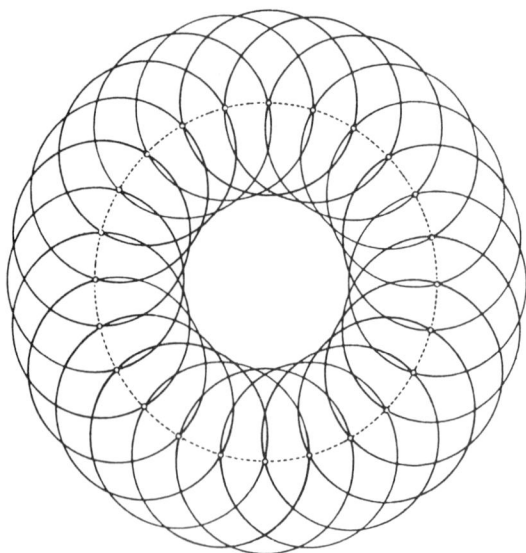

Figure 74

In Figure 75 certain areas between these circles are shown alternately in black and white. This could have been done equally in two ways, with a static or dynamic characteristic. The static presentation would bring out various stellar forms with arcs, the dynamic suggests motion as in Figure 75.

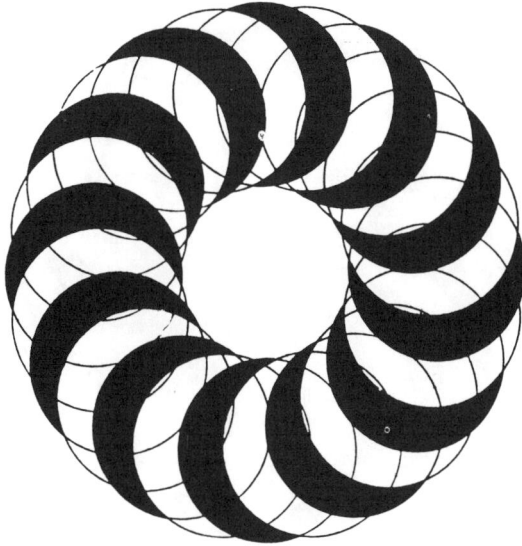

Figure 75
Rotation upon rotation

In the following diagrams, (Figure 76 and 77) the dotted circle is smaller than in the previous ones. Nevertheless, it is again divided into 24 parts. The points of division are also marked with small rings.

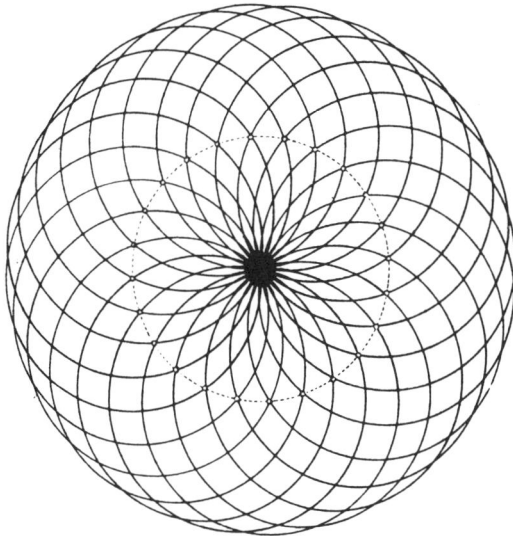

Figure 76

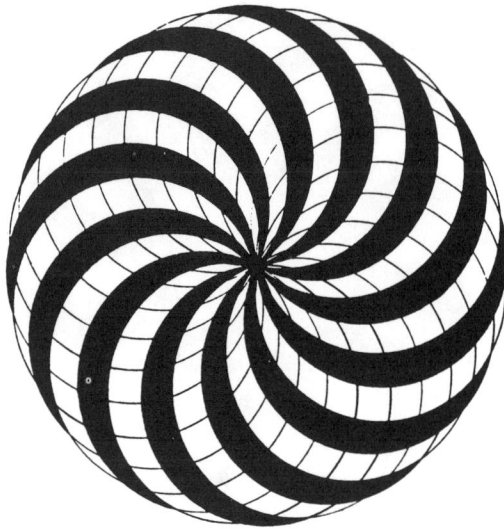

Figure 77
*The rotating circle reaches
the center*

The circles drawn around those points now reach to the center of the
dotted circle. Figure 76 shows the circles and Figure 77 emphasizes
certain areas, adding a dynamic and almost plastic impression.

In the next pair of diagrams, drawn again with a 24 division of its
dotted circle, the radius of the rotating circle reaches beyond the center of the diagram. Considering for instance the highest position of the
rotating circle, its center is at the highest point of the dotted circle and
it reaches up to the highest point of the whole diagram and down to
the lowest point of the circular space within its ring. The diagram produces a picture of a torus, a three dimentional circular ring.

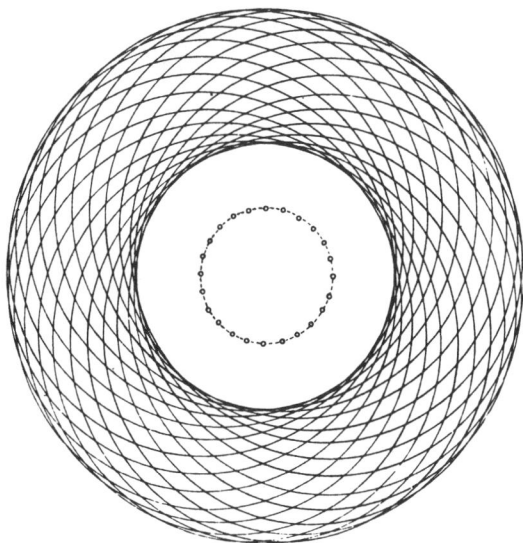

Figure 78

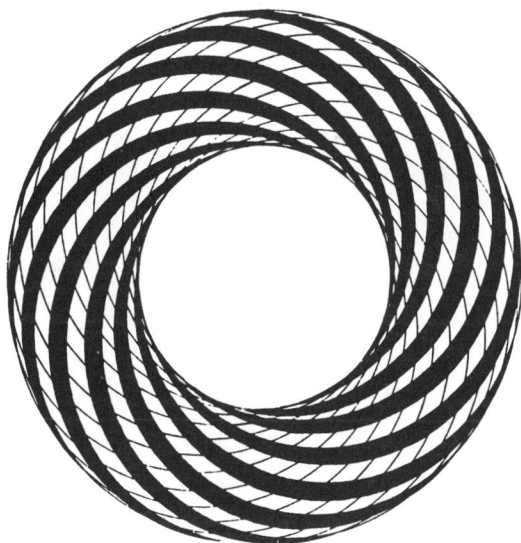

Figure 79
*The rotating circle reaches
beyond the center*

In Figure 81, a circle is once more divided into 24 parts. The points of division are connected with the lowest point on its periphery. The particular regularity of the diagram this time is not due to an equality of lengths, but of angles. All angles between neighboring lines converging to the one point are equal (proof in the footnote*).

The converging lines (with the addition of the not drawn tangent in the lowest point) form 24 angles between them. As they are equal, each angle has $180/24 = 7\frac{1}{2}°$. With a drawing-triangle one can check that an angle of 45 degrees contains six such angles, an angle of 60 degrees contains eight such angles. Nature also makes use of such diagrams in the patterns of a number of shells.

In Figure 82, not only one point has been connected with the points of the 24-division, but two points, one to the left and one to the right. (A and B).

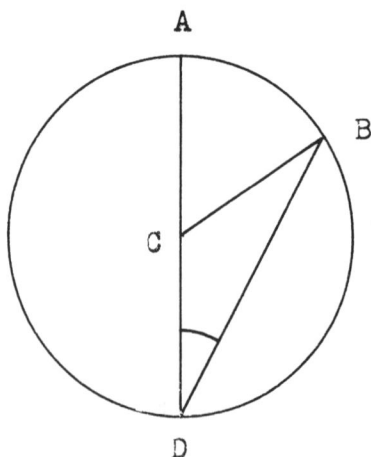

Figure 80

---

* The angle ACB is an exterior angle of the triangle BCD which is isosceles (two sides equal the radius). Therefore, half of this angle equals an angle at its base. If angle ACB increases in equal steps, the marked angle at D will also add equal steps of half its size.

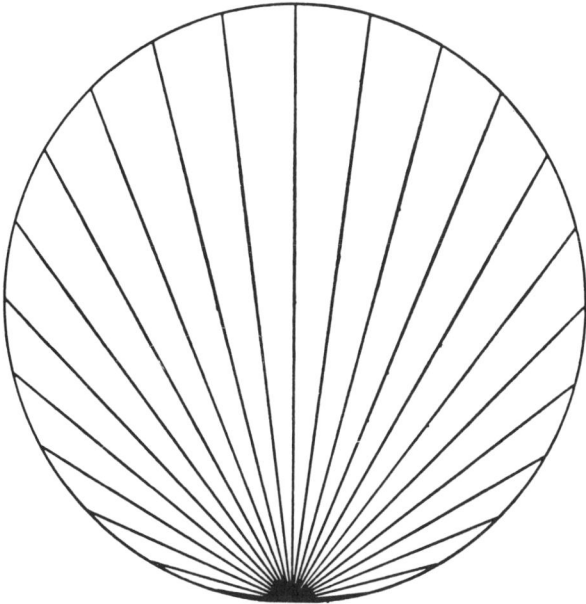

Figure 81

Inscribed angles of a circle

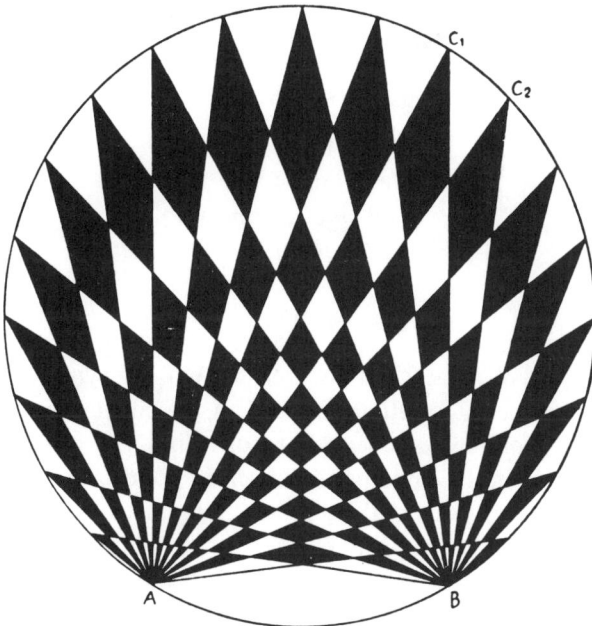

Figure 82

Two points connected with the points of the 24 Division of a circle

53

The following diagram can serve to test the skill already acquired in geometric drawing, as the points of intersection of the lines drawn to the two points of conversion lie on circles which pass through the two points of convergence (Figure 83).

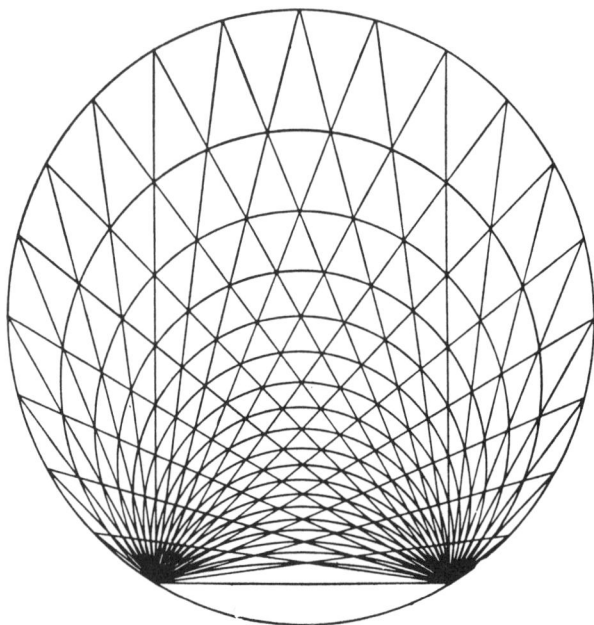

Figure 83
*The points of intersection
lie on circles passing
through the points of convergence*

Their centers are located on the vertical axis of symmetry of the diagram and at the intersection points with the converging lines. Among these intersection points one will readily find the center of the surrounding circle itself. The next intersection point below it is the center of the next circle inside and its radius is its distance from the centers of convergence. The next intersection point below it is the center of the next circle, etc. It is a diagram with a maximum of coinciding intersections.